Original title:
Oranges and Memories

Copyright © 2025 Creative Arts Management OÜ
All rights reserved.

Author: Micah Sterling
ISBN HARDBACK: 978-1-80586-448-6
ISBN PAPERBACK: 978-1-80586-920-7

The Color of Days Well Spent

In the kitchen, a fruit with a grin,
Peeling laughter, where do I begin?
Juice drips down, a sugary spree,
Mismatched socks dance, oh what glee!

Sunshine bursts in vivid hues,
Twirling with friends, we share the blues.
A zesty giggle, a citrusy fling,
Life's little tangs make our hearts sing.

We juggle the past like a circus clown,
Bellyaches rise, we're upside down.
Silly memories of stubbed toes,
And sticky fingers, who really knows?

In the garden, we chase the light,
Splitting fruit like a playful fight.
Sweet-tart moments, a lively dance,
Under the sun, we laugh at chance.

Veins of the Citrus

In a grove where laughter thrives,
Juicy secrets burst with jives.
Squirrels plot with citrus flair,
While birds critique my messy hair.

The sun shines bright, a zesty show,
As I slip on juice—Oh no!
Neighbors giggle at my fate,
I dance like I'm on a hot plate.

Laughter's Flavor

A slice of zest brings silly grins,
Each bite thinks it's a game that wins.
Juicy jokes drip from the peel,
As I trip, I just can't conceal.

In the kitchen, chaos reigns,
Fruit battle—who loses, who gains?
I juggle fruits, and they just roll,
My silly antics steal the show.

A Basket of Yesterdays

In a basket wrapped in time,
Past flavors dance, they sing their rhyme.
I recall each zesty blunder,
Like slipping on juice—what a wonder!

The days go by, the fruit still glows,
With each peel, a story flows.
I laugh again at things I've done,
A bittersweet flavor turned to fun.

Uplifted Spirits

With zest, we bounce on childhood ground,
Silly voices in the air abound.
Marshmallow dreams on citrus skies,
As we plot and laugh, oh what a surprise!

We share our chuckles, bright and bold,
A squeeze of humor—never old.
Joy floats high, it never ends,
In fruity fun, my heart ascends.

Flavors of Home in Citrus Glow

In the kitchen, scents collide,
A splash of zest, I cannot hide.
Lemon peels and giggles soar,
I'm the king of fruity lore.

Slices tossed in bowls of cheer,
Making salads, none shall fear.
Citrus games and sticky hands,
The best of childhood, laughter stands.

Luminous Tracks of Sweetness

Bouncing oranges down the hall,
The dog was quick to join the ball.
He caught one, gave a toothy grin,
Oops, there goes my orange skin!

Juicy prizes in a race,
Splattered laughter all over the place.
Chasing citrus like it's gold,
My silly antics never old.

An Ode to Sunlit Echoes

Sunshine spills on morning toast,
As zestful mornings make me boast.
With breakfast jam, I take a bite,
It's citrus magic, pure delight!

Spinning tales of fruit and rhyme,
Making pancakes feel sublime.
Whisking dreams with zestful play,
I save the best for a rainy day.

Fleeting Citrus Whispers in the Breeze

Just a whiff of tangy bliss,
Mom's secret juice, I surely miss.
Games of toss and frisbee flies,
With sticky hands and silly sighs.

Juice fights in the summer sun,
Little ones laughing, oh what fun!
As memories swirl like a fruit parade,
In every bite, a sweet charade.

Fuzzy Memories on Citrus Breezes

In fields of bright hue, I did prance,
I slipped on a peel, lost my balance.
Laughing with friends, we danced all day,
Chasing the sun, in our playful sway.

A tree with a grin, it winked at me,
Telling tall tales, how wild we could be.
Sticky fingers smear, sweet zest in the air,
Giggles echo loud, with not a single care.

The Oracle of Orange-Streaked Skies

Beneath a sunset, my dreams take flight,
Sipped juice with a twist, oh, what a sight!
The fortune teller squinted, oh so wise,
Predicting my fate with citrusy lies.

She said I'd find love, in a fruit market stall,
With a wink and a grin, I'd catch it all.
But I tripped on a rind, fell flat on my face,
And found my true love at the doctor's place.

Reflections in a Zest-Stained Mirror

In a mirror that giggles, I see my own grin,
With juice running down, it's a sticky win.
A past filled with laughter, a slip on the ground,
With zest in our hearts, joy always found.

Each squirt of sunshine adds flavor to time,
And the laughter that follows, like a bright chime.
We painted our days with the brightest of hues,
In a world full of laughter, we just could not lose.

Tracing Footsteps in Sweetness

We traced our steps on a sugary path,
With each squishy footprint, we'd burst into laughs.
The sticky adventure, so zany and bright,
With dreams that were golden, we danced through the night.

As the wind sang its tune, we'd hop like a sprite,
In a world that was merry, everything felt right.
With peals of laughter that danced in the air,
Our whimsical journey, a citrus affair.

The Orchard of Our Hearts

In the grove where laughter grows,
We swung from branches like pros.
Falling fruit, a sticky prize,
We smeared it on our little thighs.

The bees buzzed tunes, a playful dance,
While we took turns to dare a glance.
Old Granny's hat got caught in a tree,
Who knew it would look so silly on me!

Lemonade Dreams Beneath a Citrus Sun

Under the sun, we made our stand,
A pitcher filled by little hands.
Soursweets trickled down our chins,
We giggled as the day begins.

With popsicle wars and laughter loud,
We wore our sticky selves like a shroud.
The ants joined in, a tiny parade,
As we tried to find some shade.

Dancing Shadows in Twilight's Citrus Light

As shadows stretched, we stole a ride,
On our bikes down the hill we glide.
A jar of zest, our secret stash,
We'd down it quick, then make a splash.

The night would hum with friendly cheers,
When mischief whispered in our ears.
We found the glow of fireflies bright,
In their dance, we saw our flight.

Splashes of Golden Reminiscence

In the splash zone of our childhood spree,
Water balloons flew wild and free.
A hit to pass, a drenching thrill,
With giggles echoing over the hill.

Our secret treehouse, a pirate's den,
With treasure maps drawn by crazy pen.
The rules for fun were simple, clear,
Laugh and dodge — let go of fear!

Peel Back the Layers of Time

In a bowl they sit, bright and round,
Juicy tales and laughter abound.
Little pips of sunshine cheer,
Yet sticky fingers often appear.

We reminisce with every bite,
Slipping on juice, what a sight!
Grandma's cake, a citrus tease,
Always left us weak in knees.

Zesty pranks, oh what a game,
Bouncing laughter, oh the fame!
Who knew that fruits could bring such glee,
Life's a circus, come join me!

Now we ponder the days gone by,
Peeling layers under the sky.
Silly moments, bright and sweet,
Life's a fruit, can't be beat!

Sun-Kissed Tokens of the Past

A twist of zest, a hint of fun,
Chasing shadows in the sun.
Tales of snacks and silly games,
Jumping puddles, calling names.

Remember how we'd sneak a bite?
Juice dripped down, oh what a sight!
Stains on clothes, our battle scar,
With giggles echoing from afar.

Citrus smiles through silly pranks,
Hiding treasures in our ranks.
Grandpa's laughter, bright and bold,
Fruity tales forever told.

In a bowl these gems reside,
Stirring memories deep inside.
With every slice, a joke will hark,
Reminding us to laugh and spark!

Sweet and Sour Days

The zest of youth, so bright and bold,
Stories linger, never old.
Sour faces meeting sweet,
Joyful chaos on repeat.

Lemonade stands in the sun,
No buyers, still we run.
Spilled drinks and laughter loud,
Making memories with the crowd.

Sticky hands and cheeky grins,
Wagering who forages wins.
Turning fruits into delight,
Every moment feels so right.

Fruity jokes and silly cheer,
Nostalgic tastes that bring us here.
In every bite, a story spins,
Tracing joy where laughter begins!

A Garden of Forgotten Flavors

Among the leaves, a memory sits,
Plump and juicy, making hits.
Giggles ring in colorful shade,
Taste of summers, never fade.

Peeking bright through foliage green,
Nature's treats, what a scene!
Sneaky snacks and playful bites,
Making mischief under lights.

With each crunch, a laugh will bloom,
Fruity treasures fill the room.
Tales of tasting, wild and free,
Dancing dreams, oh let it be!

Keep the garden in your heart,
Where every flavor plays a part.
Sowing joy through every layer,
Life's a garden, joyous player!

Citrus Echoes

In the bowl, they roll and ride,
Mimicking laughter, side by side.
A squeeze too tight and juice does fly,
Sweet chaos reigns, oh my, oh my!

Zesty tales of days gone by,
Slipping peels, a memory's sly.
Each pucker brings a chuckle loud,
Like foolish kids who stand too proud.

Sunshine smiles and tangy glee,
Brightened minds, oh can't you see?
Visions of juice stains on the floor,
Like dancing on a citrus shore.

So here we sit, a squeezy crew,
With sticky hands and giggles too.
In laughter's grip, we all partake,
For every slice, a fun mistake!

Peel of Time

Time slips by like a juicy wedge,
With each bite, we laugh, and pledge:
To never find the perfect fruit,
Yet still we try, in relentless pursuit.

The skin flies off in a wild way,
A slippery slide on a sunny day.
With laughter echoing through the air,
The zest of life, oh, what a flare!

Each bite a giggle, each drip a chuckle,
In life's grand fruit salad, we snuggle.
Memories peel back, one by one,
Just sticky moments, oh what fun!

We gather round with sticky hands,
Creating stories that life demands.
In every taste, a whiff of cheer,
With the zest of life, we persevere!

Slices of Yesterday

A slice so bright, it makes us grin,
A frothy drink with laughs within.
We reminisce by syrupy light,
Oh, how those days were sweet and bright!

Beneath the sun's warm golden rays,
We spilled our juice in playful ways.
The fruit was ripe, the jokes were keen,
With each bite tasted, life was seen.

Chasing memories, we skip and trip,
In fruit-laden fun, we take a sip.
Each droplet shared, a giggle made,
In zesty games, our fears do fade.

So gather 'round, my fruity friends,
For every tart, a laugh ascends.
We'll juggle rounds of time and fun,
In juicy bliss, our hearts will run!

Fragrant Remnants

Underneath the tree, we play,
With citrus peels, we pave the way.
The scent that wafts brings back the past,
With messy hands, our joys amassed.

Sticky fingers, laughter loud,
Juicy moments draw a crowd.
We make a mess, when crunch gave way,
To silly antics and bright forays.

On sunny days, we dance and sing,
Joking 'bout the trials that fruit can bring.
Each little slip, a tale that's spun,
With every citrus burst, laugh till we run.

In fragrant remnants, stories abide,
As we reminisce with the fruit as our guide.
The laughter echoes, bright as night,
In our citrus world, everything feels right!

The Essence of Those Sunlit Moments

In the park, I lost a shoe,
Chasing laughter, it just flew.
Sipping juice, a sticky trend,
Splashes held, my best friend.

Sunshine spills, a giggle fest,
Squirrel feasts, ignored the rest.
Dancing with a whimsied bee,
Dictates where I wish to be.

Lemonade serenades the air,
While ants join in, so unaware.
Juggling snacks with great delight,
A bright splash of humor, just right.

In the end, pie stuck to me,
And who needs that jubilee?
Mem'ries squeeze tight, laughter's embrace,
Sunlit joy, a silly chase.

Citrus Dreams on My Tongue

Twisted straws and paper boats,
Raced on juice, with goofy quotes.
A citrus twist, I've lost my grip,
Like every time I try to sip.

Friend's wild tales of fruit escapade,
Now it's messy, then it's played.
The zesty spritz of laughter rings,
As sticky hands, the fun it brings.

We pranked the ice cream guy with zest,
He squirted lemon, we were blessed!
Oh, how those flavors danced and swirled,
In moments where delight unfurled.

Splashing juice like water guns,
Giggles echo, we had won!
A tangy tale, a silly fling,
What new weird joy tomorrow brings!

Sun-Drenched Pieces of Me

Dripping with the sweetest blend,
Juicy mishaps that won't end.
Of dance moves lost and ankle sprains,
Sun-kissed folly that remains.

Painted dreams on cheeks so bright,
The squeeze of life, a silly bite.
Boosted by laughter, cheeks aglow,
A fruity scene, with quite the show.

Jumpy jokes and zesty fun,
Giggling 'neath the blazing sun.
Each slice a chapter, bright and wild,
Who knew that I could be this child?

At sunset's edge, with stains not few,
Confection tales we'll always pursue.
Hand in hand with joy I found,
In sunny days where laughter's bound.

Faded Fronds of Lushness

Lost in a grove of fragrant dreams,
Where every fruit bursts at the seams.
A tumble, a trip, a juicy crash,
In this grove, it's all a splash.

Banana peels, my treacherous foes,
Dance of clumsiness, how it grows.
A puddle of juice, a slip and slide,
In the funhouse where giggles reside.

Chubby cheeks with juice-dripped charm,
Sweetness blooms, no cause for alarm.
Sunlight spins in fruity delight,
Even the ants join in a bite.

With wild tales of days gone by,
Each sip and story makes me sigh.
Those blushing scenes shall not decay,
In faded fronds where laughter plays.

Harvested Echoes

In a garden lined with laughter,
Where lemon trees grow bitter dreams,
I slipped on peels, a silly disaster,
As juice ran down, or so it seems.

A parrot squawked, my hat took flight,
Chasing it down was quite the sight!
I tripped on roots, my foot in the air,
The critters laughed, but I didn't care.

With friends who giggled like they were bold,
We danced around the oranges untold.
Spilled juice became our slippery floor,
We skated through fun, wanting more.

In the chaos of our sweet retreat,
Each citrus splash made life so sweet.
With sticky hands and grins so wide,
The garden's mischief was our pride.

Tangy Recollections

I found a fruit that wore a grin,
A zesty ball, all twisted skin.
I took a bite, it squirted bright,
The neighbors yelled, 'What a fright!'

Lemonade mugs turned into cheer,
With every splash, we'd holler near.
My aunt slipped in, a twisty gale,
Grumbling loud about the fail.

A picnic planned, but ants conspired,
To steal our snacks, they all retired.
We chased them down with citrus zest,
The lunch turned wild, we loved the jest.

Those days of fruit and foolery,
The laughter pours like juice, you see.
Each funny tale, a memory bright,
Eclipsed by giggles, pure delight.

Sunset Songs

The sun dipped low, in citrus flair,
With shadows playing everywhere.
A furball rolled, with zest it danced,
A swirl of fur that took a chance.

We kicked a ball, it hit the tree,
And out fell all things summery.
A fruit parade on a merry spree,
We laughed so hard, so wild and free!

The evening bloomed with citrus hues,
We sang off-key, with old-time blues.
A family of birds joined in our tune,
Swaying along to the night's bright moon.

As laughter echoed through sweet air,
My heart filled up with joy to share,
With friends and quirks, what a fine song,
These silly moments where we belong.

Citrus-Stained Nostalgia

Once, my tongue turned bright and sore,
From eating treats, I always swore.
A candy mishap, a sticky throne,
My friends still tease, 'You're well-known!'

A fruit fight broke on the sunny lawn,
Flying fruit before the dawn.
A leap, a hop, then doughy flop,
Who knew snacks could make us drop?

We'd gather round for juice and cheer,
Sipping sweetness, conquering fear.
Mishaps made us roll with glee,
Sunkissed laughter, wild and free.

Now here I sit, with old tales spun,
In sticky light, our hearts still run.
With every sip, a joke in time,
We laugh and love in every rhyme.

Sunlit Citrus Moments

In a grove where laughter grows,
Sunshine drips from heavy prose.
Juicy tales of clumsy falls,
Sticky fingers, and citrus balls.

A squirrel stole a slice or two,
Wearing zest like a bright new shoe.
Dancing bees in a frenzy swirl,
Buzzing tunes of a fragrant world.

Jumping squirrels with mischief planned,
Tumbling through a citrus land.
Rolling oranges down the street,
A juicy race that can't be beat.

Sweet slices have their own appeal,
Truths revealed in a citrus meal.
Juicy giggles fill the air,
In sunlit spheres, we find our flair.

Remnants of Tangy Days

Once a feud with a nearby lime,
Sour faces in sunny clime.
Zesty jokes and laughter spill,
As tangy tales give quite a thrill.

Rolling peels like orange hills,
A mountain of zest, oh what a thrill!
Chasing scents where sweetness roams,
In a world of juicy homes.

Picnics perched on grassy sprees,
Sipping sunshine with the bees.
Splashes of juice on cheery cheeks,
Laughter ripples—what fun it seeks!

Memories burst in every bite,
A sweet punchline to the night.
Citrus chaos, but what a game,
Each ripe moment is never the same.

Sweet Fragments in the Air

A splash of zest on summer's breath,
Tickles of sweetness, defying death.
Crazy birds on playful quests,
Squeaking tales of juicy jests.

Stumbling through a garden maze,
Hiding treats in the sun's warm rays.
Mischief tangled in sour trails,
As giggles float among the gales.

Bright spills of juice while running fast,
Tasting sunshine—who knew it'd last?
Silly stories that make us dance,
In this tangy, whimsical chance!

Fragments swirling, a burst of cheer,
In splendid snippets, we draw near.
Sunkissed laughs, the perfect blend,
Sweet aromas that twist and bend.

Tasting Time's Sunshine

Time unwinds in juicy ways,
Giggles echo through sunlit days.
Sipping bliss from citrus cups,
Finding fun in joyful ups.

Splashes of color invade the lane,
Every taste is a playful gain.
Bouncing bites with glee in tow,
Each ripe laugh, a zestful show.

Wobbling on the garden edge,
Tasting time's warmth, we take the pledge.
Squeezy giggles pop like fizz,
A tangy life—the ultimate whiz!

In a world where flavors dance,
We find time's sunshine in every chance.
Savoring sweetness, an endless rhyme,
Where laughter sparkles, tasting time.

Sun-Kissed Remembrances

In summer's glow, a fruit parade,
Juicy joys and lemon-lime charade.
A slip and slide, laughter so loud,
Silly dance moves, oh so proud.

Sticky fingers and silly grins,
Chasing the dog, dodging twin spins.
We clutched our treats, all sweet and bright,
Squeezed juice dripped, what a sight!

A tree so grand, our secret hide,
Where giggles lived, and woes would slide.
The warmth of sun, a golden hue,
With each memory, the day feels new.

So here we are, with zestful cheer,
Dancing through shadows, year after year.
Let's grab those fruits, let laughter swell,
In this bright tale, all's well that's swell.

Juicy Whispers

Beneath the twists of leafy crowns,
We'd huddle close, avoiding frowns.
The ticking clock, a naughty tease,
Time drips slow, like honeyed breeze.

We'd gather round with joyful flare,
Bold flavors matched with childhood dare.
Spitting seeds, we took our aim,
Giggles echoed, never tame.

Shorts and sneakers, wild as can be,
This fruity fling was pure glee.
The tongue-twisting tales we spun,
Whispers of laughter, joy, and fun.

So here's to days where fruit meets play,
A cocktail of joy in a sunlit ray.
Juicy delights, a crazy scene,
In our hearts forever, they gleam.

The Aroma of Youth

Freshly peeled with zestful flair,
We'd trade our secrets, light as air.
The smell of sun, with mischief bold,
A treasure chest of tales unfolds.

Ripe tales mingled with laughter's tune,
Cartwheels spun under a lazy moon.
We'd sneak those bites, our cheeks so wide,
With each sweet burst, a silly slide.

Picking fruit while avoiding chores,
Daring each other, opening doors.
Sticky situations, giggles ensued,
Filled with fun, and that carefree mood.

With every slice, a new delight,
Bouncing back to those carefree nights.
Savor the scent, let laughter beam,
In this zesty world, we still dream.

Golden Reflections

In the golden glow of carefree days,
We'd compete in our extra-gross ways.
Orange stains on shirts, what a treat,
Each pitfall, crafted with wild feat.

Racing down hills with sticky hands,
We dared each other, made silly plans.
Footraces ended in spontaneous falls,
Orange confetti lit up our calls.

And in the heat, we'd gather 'round,
Sharing secrets that knew no bounds.
Sunny chats and fruitful schemes,
A slice of youth, wrapped in dreams.

So lift your juice, toast with glee,
To the laughter shared and the wild spree.
In memories bright, we're still alive,
With sunny smiles, we shall thrive!

Citrus Sunsets and Heartbeats

In a grove where laughter grows,
A fruit fell down and landed close.
It bounced and rolled, as if alive,
Chasing squirrels, it took a dive.

Juicy splats on life's great stage,
Sending giggles, turning page.
A sticky hand, a toothy grin,
Oh, how the citrus dance begins!

A bright orange zest in the air,
As bumblebees sing without a care.
Chasing rainbows, ripe and round,
Who knew such joy could be found?

In twilight beams, we eat and laugh,
With every slice, a silly gaffe.
Who knew a fruit could inspire cheer,
While we swap tales and sip our beer?

Bright Echoes from a Honeyed Past

Once upon a time, we'd play,
With squishy treats on a sunny day.
A pebble hit a fruity prize,
And suddenly we had surprise!

Laughter bubbled like a drink,
As we leaned back and began to think.
About sticky hands and sweet teeth,
And all the joy that life bequeath.

In a fruit fight, we took our stand,
Chased by friends, just like a band.
A splash of juice, a burst of fun,
Before the day was all but done.

We share the tales, we drape in cheer,
With funny fruits that dance, oh dear!
The echoes ring, like bells of gold,
In this sweet tale, we're feeling bold!

Serendipity in Citrusy Hues

In the market, colors blend,
Each hue turns tides, and moods transcend.
One gleaming fruit caught my eye,
And made me giggle at its sly.

I tossed it high, it soared away,
Rolled down the path, a zesty play.
Each bounce a burst of giggling sound,
And on our faces, joy is found.

The sights and sounds, a random spree,
With each small drop, sweet jubilee.
We laughed so hard, neighbors did stare,
At a simple fruit, we had our share!

In the end, with juice on our chin,
We shared our secrets, and all within.
What joy we find in the playful hue,
Of fruity fragments, just me and you!

The Radiance of Forgotten Laughter

Underneath the evening sky,
We tossed around memories, oh my!
A wedge of joy, we'd never cease,
Found laughter bursting - oh, sweet release!

The sticky moments, tales retold,
Like tasty treasures of new and old.
A wobbly moment, a fruit a-fly,
Filling our hearts, we giggled high.

Sipping drinks that shimmer bright,
With every sip, we take delight.
In mishaps, we find our grand design,
Where happiness and sweetness intertwine.

So raise your glass, let laughter lift,
These fruity fantasies, our greatest gift!
For in each slice, we find our way,
To joyous nights and brighter days!

A Mosaic of Fragrant Yesterdays

In the market of laughter, we'd roam,
Picking odd fruit that tasted like foam.
Juicy secrets dripped down our chins,
As we munched on the joy, let the madness begin.

Sticky fingers, a treasure so bright,
Slurping and giggling, a delightful sight.
Grandma's stash had a magical scent,
Making us wish that these moments be lent.

The neighbor's dog thought we were a feast,
Chasing us down, acting like a beast.
Running away, we'd twirl and we'd twine,
Squeezing our snacks in the warm sunshine.

Now we reminisce, with a chuckle and grin,
Of fruity adventures that still make us spin.
Life's sweetest episodes slip through our hands,
Yet those goofy days are our favorite strands.

The Glow of Childhood Smiles

In the corner of summer, we'd collide,
With giggles and grins that couldn't hide.
Two silly kids on a trip to delight,
Finding mischief, even in twilight.

We'd bake goofy pies with splashes of zest,
Muddling flavors, no time to rest.
Lemon and lime turned into a fight,
For a slice of laughter, oh what a sight!

In the glow of the sunset, oh how we'd dance,
Lost in the moment, a fanciful trance.
Dreams dipped in syrup, we tasted the sun,
Frolicsome moments, we'd shout, "We've won!"

Now stories of laughter and fruit blend well,
In our silly hearts, where pure joy will dwell.
With hugs made of citrus and joy as our guide,
We cherish those times, where our worries subside.

Under the Shade of Citrus Leaves

Beneath the grand tree, we'd plot and we'd scheme,
Crafting wild tales like girls in a dream.
The tangy aroma filled all the air,
With giggles so loud, it made the birds stare.

We sculpted strange crowns from the fruit's sunny shade,
Creating a kingdom where mischief had played.
Royal decrees made with of giggles and cheer,
"From this moment forth, dessert's on the pier!"

Our treasure map led us on quests full of glee,
Pirates of laughter, as bold as could be.
Dodging the veggies, we'd claim our long prize,
Life was a banquet beneath the blue skies.

Now we gather 'round, recounting old days,
When silliness blossomed in fanciful ways.
With tales of delight that never grow old,
We smile at the gold that these memories hold.

When Life Gave Us Sun

We danced in the warmth with a bounce in our step,
Seeking bright moments as laughter leapt.
The world was our stage, under skies painted gold,
In a cauldron of fun, we were brave and bold.

With sticky sweet treasures, we'd barter and trade,
The flavor of joy in the games that we played.
Our hands were all yellow, our hearts filled with light,
In this carnival of life, everything felt right.

Fallen fruit battles, we launched with a grin,
As juice dripped down noses, the laughter slipped in.
Life tossed us sunshine, we caught every ray,
Turning every day's troubles to bright cabaret!

Now as we linger and sip on our drink,
We laugh at the past with a nod and a wink.
Every little bite of that sweetness we crave,
Is a sprinkle of fun in the laughter we save.

The Luminescence of Child's Play

In the glow of summer skies,
We chased the winds with silly cries.
A splash of juice, a burst of glee,
Caught in laughter, wild and free.

Our childhood games, so bright and bold,
Collecting treasures, tales retold.
Sticky fingers, sunny stains,
Dancing through our silly lanes.

The world a canvas, wide and bright,
With every giggle, pure delight.
We spun like tops, with giddy grace,
Worn-out shoes, a joyful race.

Yet here we stand with puzzled looks,
Recalling sweetness from our books.
Why were we mad to laugh and play?
Oh, the joys of yesterday!

Harvesting Heartstrings

In gardens where our laughter grows,
We plucked the fruit, forgot the woes.
Each bite, a burst, a flavor fest,
Bestowed by nature, oh so blessed!

Sticky tales of summer's bliss,
A mischief done, a stolen kiss.
With fruit punch dreams and silly schemes,
Our laughter spilled like sunny streams.

We'd race the clouds and dream of soar,
Fields of mirth behind each door.
Yet memories fade like shadows cast,
Around the corners of our past.

Caught in a whim, the jug was cracked,
Mom's favorite recipe, we hacked!
The flavors wild, like days gone by,
With every giggle, we reach for the sky!

Radiant Echoes of Citrus Delight

A splash of zest in summer's beam,
We lived a fruity, silly dream.
Startling grins, and wobbly knees,
Crafting chaos, if you please!

With every crunch, our joy displayed,
Caught in the sunlight, unafraid.
We danced like fruit flies, light and spry,
A burst of laughter, oh my, oh my!

We'd toss the peels with grinning eyes,
While plotting mischief, just for laughs.
Memories like seeds, they scatter wide,
Chasing the echoes of our pride.

Remember the time, we lost the fight?
A fruit fight grand—what pure delight!
Oh, we were so sticky, but who would care?
With giggles and play, we filled the air!

Tasting the Warmth of Days Lost

Remember when we chased the sun,
In fields of laughter, oh what fun!
The warmth of days we'd gobble up,
With sticky hands and a full cup.

Where sunshine spilled like sweetened juice,
Together making our own excuse.
The world our stage, where we performed,
In citrus dreams, we all conformed.

The flavor of youth still lingers near,
Each goofy act brings back the cheer.
As seasons dance, we chase the zest,
And grasp the moments we love best.

So here's to sunshine and all we share,
In the tapestry of life, unaware.
Each bite, a toast to times we found,
The joys of youth, forever abound!

Resplendent Reflections in Orange

In the garden, a mishap of peels,
Slipping and sliding, oh what squeals!
A citrus grin upon each face,
As we dance and juggle in this place.

A cat sneezed loud, oh what a show,
Chasing sunshine—where did it go?
Lemons roll, and laughter erupts,
As we share our fruity cup-ups.

Sticky hands from a juicy bite,
Splatters of zest, oh what delight!
We tell tall tales of days gone by,
While fruity scents drift up to the sky.

Our treasure trove of silly chats,
Gifts unwrapped, in colorful hats.
With each slice, a story grows,
In our hilarious oranges, joy flows.

Sweet Sunbeams in Jars

We caught the sun in a big glass jar,
And laughed at the light, oh how bizarre!
Like butterflies trapped in our glee,
Flashing smiles as bright as can be.

A picnic spread near wobbly chairs,
Sweet stumbles dance through morning airs.
In spinny circles, we did revolve,
Chasing giggles that won't dissolve.

Jelly spills on the kitchen floor,
Turned into art we can't ignore.
Brushes and spoons, a painter's delight,
Creating chaos in the soft daylight.

We untwist memories like candy gold,
Each one sweeter as the day unfolds.
With every bite, we recount our charms,
In sweet sunbeams, life's in our arms.

The Weight of Golden Slices

Counting slices stacked too high,
Juggling fruit with a gleeful sigh.
A plummeting piece, oh what a crash,
A citrus joke in a splendid splash.

Giggles enhance our fruity feast,
Each bite a giggle, laughter's beast.
Pillow fights of peels everywhere,
With sticky fingers, no soul would care.

Sitting in piles of joyful zest,
Finding treasures in the very best.
We trade winks and hilarious tricks,
In our taste of summer, laughter sticks.

Time bends like a silly twist,
Chasing the juice that can't be missed.
With the weight of slices in our hands,
We declare our kingdom—citrus lands.

Twilight Whiffs of Time

As twilight dances on the lawn,
A fruity scent lingers, whispers dawn.
We toss our worries with a zestful cheer,
Laughter bubbles, the end is near.

Stargazing with a splash of fun,
Biting into tales when day is done.
Each spark of chatter carries a glow,
In this sunset, our laughter flows.

Catching echoes in the cool night air,
Fruity aromas lead us somewhere.
We stumble through stories, a zestful ride,
With every giggle, our hearts collide.

In the quiet, sweet dreams ignite,
Of citrus moments, framing the night.
As time drips slowly with juicy delight,
We cherish the laughs, wrapped up tight.

Blushing Hues of Affection

In a bowl, they giggle bright,
With peels that catch the morning light.
A fruit parade of yellow cheer,
Each slice a laugh, each wink a tear.

I took a bite, a juicy jest,
And squirted juice – oh, what a mess!
My shirt now boasts a citrus stain,
A wearable tale of zestful gain.

Friends all gathered, laughter grows,
As citrus slips amidst the prose.
We muse on life's peculiar swings,
And find joy in the silly things.

In sunlit rooms, our chatter rolls,
As fragrant peels reveal their souls.
With zest and glee, the memories blend,
In every slice, a spoken trend.

Glassy Reflections in a Citrus Bowl

A shiny bowl upon the table,
It holds a treasure, oh so stable.
With shiny orbs of sunny hue,
They claim to laugh, if only true!

I tried to juggle, what a sight!
One slipped away into the night.
It rolled beneath the chair so sly,
And then returned with a citrus sigh.

A zesty scent fills up the air,
I dance around without a care.
With every toss, a memory flies,
Of days gone by, with jolly cries.

The glassy bowl reflects our joys,
Like playful cats, like eager boys.
And every slip brings laughter's goal,
In this bright space, we share our soul.

Juicy Auras of Lost Warmth

A sunny day, we clamor loud,
With juicy bites, we draw a crowd.
Each segment tells a tale so sweet,
With every chew, a dance, a feat.

But oops! A splash upon my face,
A sticky smile, a fruity grace.
I laugh so hard, I lose my grip,
And half my fruit goes for a trip!

We chase the peel, it slips away,
In sunlight's glow, we laugh and play.
The breezy aura catches us,
With every bite, it turns to fuss.

In sticky hands, our stories cling,
Of laughter shared and silly things.
With each burst, our spirits bloom,
In fruity warmth, we share the room.

Memories in a Zesty Infusion

A punch of zest, a citrus fling,
In playful chaos, we take wing.
The laughter flows like lemonade,
In sunny hues, our worries fade.

With every sip, a memory spins,
Of funny hats, and playful sins.
We toast to life with vibrant cheer,
And dance around without a fear.

But then a splash, it steals the show,
A juicy jest we all bestow.
We laugh until we cannot breathe,
In tangy tales, our hearts believe.

So raise your cup of zesty glee,
In silly moments, we are free.
With every drop, a smile we sown,
In vibrant tales, we're never alone.

The Zest of Old Tales

In a grove where laughter grew,
Old friends would gather, just a few.
Each peel a story, juicy and bright,
Tales of mischief, shared with delight.

Fumbling harvests, fruit on the ground,
Slip on a peel, tumbling 'round.
We scrambled and giggled, what a sight!
Nature's confetti, all day and night.

Remember the time the dog took a bite?
We chased him 'round with all of our might.
The fruit was the prize of that silly race,
Laughter echoing, time can't erase.

So let's toast with our drinks, a cheerful cheer,
To zesty moments we hold dear.
For in this orchard, the past comes alive,
With every chuckle, our spirits thrive.

Bittersweet Chapters

Under the sun, we sat by a pile,
Of past mistakes and that famous smile.
We juggled our fruits with hands full of jokes,
Like citrus comedians, the life of folks.

Each segment a laugh, each tear a giggle,
Reminders of times we'd all dance and wiggle.
Our sticky fingers, a point of pride,
Caught in the sweetness, mischief our guide.

When life threw us curves, we made some pie,
Baking with beets just to try and fly.
We conquered the kitchen, the laughter ran high,
Spitting the seeds while we aimed for the sky.

Now we write pages of ridiculous plight,
A book full of blunders, all pure delight.
With zest in our hearts and joy in our eyes,
Even mishaps can be a grand surprise!

Citrus-Laden Dreams

In dreams where the sun takes a bow,
We danced with the fruit like a circus cow.
Bouncing on segments with playful flair,
All while the cat judged us from the chair.

We wore crowns made of zest, a sticky delight,
Pretending we ruled in a kingdom of bite.
The laughter erupted with every misstep,
As we flailed and we fumbled, our own little prep.

Each citrus adventure started so sweet,
Until one found the juicer, with lightning-fast feet.
We swam in a pool of the bright and the fun,
All was well until we melted in the sun.

But who needs to worry about sticky floors?
In dreams we embrace all our wild, goofy roars.
Tomorrow we'll wake up, with pulp in our hair,
Still giggling at tales only we could declare.

Remnants of a Radiant Day

The sun painted shadows, so lively and bold,
We feasted on fun, in stories retold.
With rinds on our heads, we pranced about,
The joy of each moment, we'd never doubt.

Games of toss and catch in the golden glow,
A wayward slice took a tumble, oh no!
But laughter ensued, like a sweet serenade,
Our silly exploits, a joyous parade.

Sticky fingers and cheeks, oh, what a sight,
Each burst of flavor brought sheer delight.
So we gathered our laughter, put it on display,
Savoring the echoes of our carefree play.

As dusk drew its curtain, and day turned to night,
We clutched our treasures, all sparkly and bright.
For the remnants of joy in our hearts would stay,
Mingling like flavors, in a whimsical way.

Fleeting Harvests

In the garden, fruits so bright,
Lemons grin and apples bite.
Pick a fruit, what a delight,
Slip and slide, a comical sight.

Juggling pears, I lose my hold,
Fruits like treasure, yet so bold.
Every splash, a tale retold,
Laughter echoes, joy uncontrolled.

A basket spills, I chase it down,
Chasing figs all over town.
Silly faces, no one frowns,
In this fruity, foolish crown.

Pies on windows, laughter's call,
Sticky hands and sweet fruit brawl.
Cherished times, we have it all,
In this harvest, we will fall.

Orchard of the Past

Under trees where shadows play,
Sticky hands in bright array.
Tasting juice like kids at play,
All my troubles fade away.

Memories stuck like jam,
Laughter bursting, oh what a slam!
Chasing friends like a wild ram,
Lemonade dreams in grandma's plan.

Snapshots flash, a golden glee,
Mischief greets me, oh so free.
Every fruit, a memory spree,
Bouncing like a honeybee.

Days of sun dipped in sweet cheer,
Nothing but friends and fresh air here.
Each little bite brings us near,
Laughter ringing loud and clear.

Sweet Juxtaposition

Bananas slipping, toes all bare,
Watermelons fly through the air.
Tangy bites, a fruity affair,
Lemon's laugh, oh what a dare!

Under suns that made us glow,
Pineapple hats in a funny show.
Chasing cherries, oh so slow,
Giggling loudly, just let it flow.

Swirling fruits in a silly dance,
Twirling round, a dashing glance.
Lost in wonder, not a chance,
Life's a fruit, let's take a chance!

Jams and jellies, crafty delight,
With every splash, we bound in flight.
Joy and laughter, shining bright,
Fruity chaos, pure delight.

Days in Sunlight

Sunshine spills on leaves of green,
Marmalade skies, what a scene!
Painting moments, fresh and clean,
With laughter bursting at the seam.

Silly picnics on blankets wide,
Sipping nectar, friends beside.
Every bite, a joyful ride,
In the shade, where giggles hide.

Water fights and fruit galore,
Picking treasures from the floor.
Every taste, we ask for more,
Moments like these, we adore.

Childhood whispers on the breeze,
Frolicking with such great ease.
Laughter blooms like buzzing bees,
Living life, oh how it frees!

The Color of Remembrance

In a world of zest, we roam,
With citrus smiles, we call it home.
Every laugh like a burst, a pop,
Sweetness lingers, we never stop.

Bouncing through the sunny days,
With sticky hands and silly ways.
We danced 'neath trees with fruit so round,
Juicy chaos all around.

Thoughts sour like those left behind,
Yet in our hearts, the laughter's kind.
With every peel, a chuckle grows,
In the warmth of memories, joy flows.

So let's embrace this citrus cheer,
With every sip, we hold it dear.
Life's a fruit, take a big bite,
Let's savor flavors, feel the light.

Pulp and Past Pages

Pages turned with citrus ink,
Where giggles dance and think.
We scribbled dreams under a tree,
None so grand, but all carefree.

In sticky summers, we'd collide,
Splashes of juice where dreams reside.
Each laughter echoing like a bell,
In pulpy worlds, we knew so well.

Under sunlit skies we'd race,
Chasing moments, a zany pace.
With every slip, our spirits soared,
Memories shared, forever adored.

So let's remember each delight,
In juicy tales, we find our light.
With every splash, our lives compile,
In laughter's warmth, we reconcile.

Sunset Citrus Reflections

As the day ends in a burst,
We laugh as we quench our thirst.
Sunset hues upon our skin,
Citrus bliss fits right in.

Sliding down the golden slide,
Chasing the tide, we laugh, we hide.
Each burst of laughter tastes so sweet,
In our hearts, we feel the heat.

With memories that peel away,
A zesty glee is here to stay.
Days unfurl like juicy tape,
In every twist, a happy shape.

So pull up a chair and stay awhile,
Let's share our tales with a big smile.
As sunsets greet the night with cheer,
In every wink, our youth draws near.

Juicy Echoes of Youth

Oh, to be young with zestful dreams,
Crafting fun from silly schemes.
Sticky fingers and grinning glee,
Echoes of joy, wild and free.

We'd run through fields, laughter unbound,
With each little splash, joy profound.
In citrus skies, our tales would swirl,
Each giggle a treasure, a vibrant pearl.

Dancing in circles, we'd toss our care,
Fruit-flavored wishes hung in the air.
Every chunk of joy we'd consume,
Filling our hearts with vivid bloom.

So let's toast to the times gone by,
With juicy moments that never die.
In each burst, we find our roots,
In laughter's embrace, life's sweetest fruits.

Zestful Days Gone By

In a garden, sunlit and bright,
We'd nibble on fruit, pure delight.
With sticky hands and grins so wide,
The juice dripped down, oh what a ride!

Laughter echoed, kids on the run,
Chasing after that sweet, ripe fun.
Little feet in a careless dance,
Creating chaos at every chance.

We'd trade our treasures, scents to share,
Hidden secrets found here and there.
Conversations sweet with giggles stored,
In the playgrounds where laughter soared.

Years have flown on giggly wings,
But the taste of joy still softly sings.
Days of bursting, zesty delight,
Will forever glow, both day and night.

Fragrant Recollections of Summer

Underneath the sunny sky,
We'd play until the day said bye.
With crumbs of snacks upon our chin,
Every moment sparked a grin!

Picnics with laughter never fail,
Adventures that would always trail.
A fruit-fueled race, who'd win the prize?
But sticky fingers were our disguise.

We'd climb those trees to taste the air,
And whisper secrets, none to spare.
It's hard to fathom how time flew,
With laughter loud and friendships true.

Now I glance back, a sunny view,
With scents of cheerful breezes, too.
Each thought's a taste of summer fun,
Where joy and warmth could never shun.

Golden Halos of Laughter

In the sunshine, smiles would sprout,
Days filled with chatter, never a drought.
A playful toss of citrus gleams,
And giggles spilled like sugary streams.

Happiness hung in fragrant air,
As we danced without a care.
With every bop and little twist,
A joyful hug, how could we resist?

Pineapple hats on summer's throne,
Creators of mischief, we'd never moan.
Our wild imaginations would gleam,
A whimsical world, electric dream!

Though time flies fast, we still embrace,
Those golden days we can't replace.
For in each laugh that life bestows,
Are cherished moments in sweet repose.

The Taste of Yesterday's Glow

In shady spots, tales would unfold,
With vibrant hues and flavors bold.
We'd bite through laughter, zest divine,
And sip the sunshine, feeling fine.

Every mishap a tale to tell,
While sticky sweet was life's own spell.
The half-peeled fruit, a daring game,
With pulpy smiles and silly fame.

Days baked golden, balmy bright,
Where joy was brewed, pure delight.
Sketches in memories, wild and free,
Each taste a promise, a tapestry.

Years may fade but we'll treasure,
The golden glow of sweetened pleasure.
With every chuckle, we'll proudly show,
The zest of life's delightful flow.

Fruitful Ghosts

In an orchard where laughter began,
Ghosts dance with fruit in each hand.
They tell tales of snacks, sticky and sweet,
With juice on their faces, it's quite the treat.

One stumbled and fell, into a pie,
A creamy green filling, oh my, oh my!
They giggled and grinned, all covered in goo,
Who knew fruit could cause such a to-do?

On branches, they swing, like children at play,
Chasing the birds that tease them all day.
With every lost bite, a chuckle escapes,
In this fruity realm where the past takes shape.

So come and join in their fruity parade,
Where memories jive and never will fade.
With laughter and flavor, they're never alone,
These spectral orchard friends, in their juicy zone.

Rind and Recollection

At the market, a ghost with a cap,
Is haggling prices, oh what a trap!
He says, 'This one's sweet, though it looks a bit bruised,'
With a wink, he knows he won't be refused.

Carts rolling by with a thunderous sound,
While shadows of snacks swirl all around.
He spots a ripe melon, bright and round,
And bursts into song, a fruit-loving clown.

Neighbors all laugh, "What's he got in his sack?"
Secrets of sweetness spill from his pack.
A slice here and there, each bite's a delight,
As ghosts share their treats, all through the night.

With trays piled high, they toast and they cheer,
Every bite savored, no need for a beer.
In this sticky scene, they're quite the sight,
Rind and recollection mix wrong and right.

Lush Days Gone By

In summer's embrace, the laughter was loud,
We'd swing on the swings, in a sunbeam cloud.
With a zesty citrus, we'd shoot for the stars,
Making plans to steal fruit from the neighbor's car.

A heist so grand, we'd plot by the tree,
With flashlights and whispers, how sneaky we'd be!
But every attempt ended up with a splat,
As citrusy chaos brought us off track.

We'd munch on our spoils, sticky hands bold,
In those golden days, pure memories told.
We'd laugh at our blunders, the juicy mishaps,
As sweet laughter echoed, in memory's laps.

Those lush days roll by, a vintage delight,
With echoes of giggles that last through the night.
Each bite is a postcard, each laugh a rewind,
A fruity adventure, joyfully defined.

Blossom and Burden

Under the blooms, where the silly ones play,
An orchard of giggles awaits every day.
With pies full of splats, and apples that leap,
The blossoms bear secrets, too funny to keep.

A stumble, a tumble, then laughter galore,
As fruit flies around like it's all indoor.
'What's this on my shirt?' one girl cries with glee,
A smushed berry heart, making history.

The bloom of the fun leads us straight to the core,
Where memories grow, like fruit forevermore.
Every bite holds a story, each bellyache, too,
A burden of laughter we all must pursue.

So raise up a toast, to the joy and the mess,
With blossoms and burdens, we're feeling so blessed.
In this whimsical orchard, our spirits will soar,
With laughter and sweetness, who could ask for more?

Carving Juicy Portraits in Time

In a grove with bright smiles,
Juicy jokes hang like fruit,
Squeezing laughter from sun,
Memories roll like citrus brutes.

Sticky fingers and bright peels,
A slip on a peel brings giggles,
We juggle zest with our meals,
Laughter bursts like sweet tickles.

Rows of sunlit delight,
Each bite a burst of cheer,
We dance in the golden light,
Childhood calls, always near.

In every slice a story,
With humor we find our stance,
Life's tartness is less hoary,
As we laugh and twirl and prance.

Fields of Citrus Laughter

Among the trees, we frolic,
Witty banter fills the air,
Bouncing jokes and fruity logic,
Like confetti, we share.

A tree with zesty bellyaches,
Each giggle grows on branches,
We dodge the juice that makes haste,
In daily, silly dances.

The sun shines bright on our pranks,
Rolling on the ground we lie,
With every laugh, our joy ranks,
In fields where days just fly.

Slicing through our silly thoughts,
A fruit fight breaks the calm,
As we laugh and get all caught,
Moments sweet as summer's balm.

Tang and Time Entwined

With a twist and a grin,
We sip the tang of the day,
Tasting each moment within,
Wishing boring times away.

Champion of citrus puns,
Every slip fuels our play,
Like sunshine, laughter runs,
Making past blues fade away.

Time dances in the zest,
As we juggle joy and care,
A fruit bowl's warm, sunny nest,
Filled with giggles we all share.

Toasting with drinks of glee,
Life never feels so fine,
With every chuckle and spree,
We're bright and sharp like a rind.

Peeling Back Yesterday's Layers

In the market's bustling charm,
We peel back tales of delight,
Every strip tells a yarn,
With humor, we take flight.

Our childhoods wrapped in laughter,
Like citrus skins, full of zest,
Each punchline a sweet after,
When fun is at its best.

Slicing through the daily grind,
Juicy bits splatter and fly,
We share winks and the blind,
As the past floats like sweet pie.

So here we are, near and dear,
With smiles that always gleam,
Peeling laughter, year by year,
Life's a fruity, funny dream.

Essence of a Lost Afternoon

In the sun we played, oh what a scene,
Chasing shadows while trying to glean.
With a twist and a toss, our laughter soared,
Under the trees, sweet treasures stored.

We spilled juice on shirts, a bright orange glow,
Sticky fingers made all the fun flow.
Each giggle a marker, a time we could save,
In daydreams, our antics dance in a wave.

A squirt here, a splash there, what a delight,
Messy adventures, pure joy in our sight.
With friends all around, life felt just right,
Oh, to relive those moments, such a delight!

As shadows grew long, we raced with the sun,
A treasure of laughter, never to shun.
Hands raised in triumph, we crowned our play,
In this lost afternoon, we found our way.

Juicy Threads in a Tapestry of Life

A fruit bowl stood proud, a sight to behold,
Colors of sunshine, bright glimmers of gold.
Each slice a story, a quirky mishap,
Juices splattered, with laughter's sweet clap.

Grandma would giggle, a pie on her knee,
"Just don't eat it all, or you won't taste the tree!"
We'd nod in agreement while stuffing our face,
Creating our chaos, not caring of grace.

From juice mustaches to gooey delight,
In snack time adventures, we danced day and night.
With every tossed slice, we'd burst into glee,
Painting our moments with zest and esprit.

And when autumn came, we gathered in cheer,
For flavors of childhood always brought near.
A tapestry woven from laughter and fun,
So many bright threads, but never too done.

Fables of a Fruitful Past

In the backyard, a saga unfolds,
A battle of wits with tales of old gold.
With helmets of rind, we'd charge with a grin,
In quests for the sweetest, let the games begin!

A slice here, a wedge there, we fought for our share,
The juicy bounty, not a moment to spare.
'Watch out!', we'd yell, as we dodged a ripe fling,
Turning snack time into a wild, silly fling.

Each seed was a whisper, a secret from youth,
Of playful debates and the joys of truth.
With laughter as currency, we traded our tales,
In a carnival of flavors, where nobody fails.

The stories still echo in heartbeats of joy,
Of splashes and giggles, of girls and a boy.
Here's to the tales that brighten our casts,
In the chapters of life, fables of a past.

Beneath the Zest of Time

Time dripped down slow, like nectar divine,
With each fruity bite, the moments align.
A burst of delight, a tickle of tart,
In the cycles of laughter, we played our sweet part.

Sticky sweet jokes, like a carnival ride,
With sprinkles of chaos, we laughed and we cried.
With every bright harvest, a new tale began,
Beneath the zest, there's always a plan.

We'd barter our stories, our laughs and our glee,
Sharing the secrets of life's jubilee.
With laughter like juice, our spirits take flight,
In this orchard of joy, everything feels right.

So here's to the moments, the fun we embraced,
In the tangy adventure of time, we are laced.
For life's sweetest treasure, we keep close at hand,
Are memories wrapped tight in joy's brilliant band.

Slices of Sunlit Remembrance

A fruit stand winks with a sunny grin,
Juicy jokes spill, where laughter begins.
Peels tossed in air, like bright confetti,
Squeezed memories burst, oh so petty!

A splash of juice on the cheek, what fun,
Chasing the sweetness, we always run.
The tilt of a slice, a giggle or two,
Life's silly moments, in shades of bright hue.

Picking up laughter from ground like a prize,
Sunbeams and chuckles, oh how they rise!
Pithy puns shared under warm, golden rays,
Time flies like fruit flies on sunny days!

Caught in the zest of a whimsical breeze,
We juggle the joy, with the greatest of ease.
Tasting the sunshine, so sweet and so bold,
In this orchard of laughter, our tales unfold.

Tangy Nostalgia in Sunbeams

Churning up memories like a fruit smoothie,
Sipping on laughter, feeling all groovy.
The tang of the past, a tickling tune,
Under the shimmering, playful afternoon.

With giggles cascading like juice from a squeeze,
We dance in the sunshine, wrapped in the breeze.
Lost in the laughter of wild, silly games,
Reliving our youth, without any shame.

Sun-drenched recollections in bright, juicy notes,
We slip on our peels and we dance like goats.
A citrusy chuckle, we twirl and we sway,
Who knew that nostalgia could be such a play?

Threading through memories, so playful and light,
In orchards of joy, our spirits take flight.
We twinkle like seeds, each story a gem,
In the bright, zesty glow, we find who we've been.

The Aroma of Forgotten Days

A fragrance wafts by like a giggling child,
Tickling our noses, invigorated, wild.
Whispering stories in the warm summer air,
Of days baked in laughter, without a care.

Crimson sunsets burst like a funny surprise,
Laughter ricochets in the wide-open skies.
Sticky fingers fumbled, a slapstick affair,
Sunkissed and grinning, we float without care.

The scent of sweet joy in a moment caught,
Where sunshine and humor blend nicely in pot.
Kitchen antics spill over old wooden floors,
In echoes of giggles, the spirit restores.

Gathering laughter like ripe fruit from trees,
Remembering mishaps with giggles and wheeze.
Tasting the essence of times filled with cheer,
In a fragrant embrace, we gladly draw near.

Citrus Whispers Beneath the Skin

Peeling back layers, the laughter erupts,
Beneath all the surface, the silliness erupts.
Each slice of the past dusted sweet with delight,
As we reminisce under moon's glowing light.

Fruits of our youth ride the back of our smiles,
We jog down the path of our merriest miles.
With splashes and quirks, like juice in the air,
The warmth of the moments we're eager to share.

In this orchard of chuckles, we gather and sway,
Twirled up in the joy, we swing and we play.
The zest on our tongues, a dance quite unplanned,
Wrapped up in the sunbeams, laughing hand in hand.

Forever these tidbits of joy will remain,
Sparkling like sunshine, like drops of the rain.
In zealous embrace, we'll always recall,
These whispers of joy that still tickle us all.

www.ingramcontent.com/pod-product-compliance
Lightning Source LLC
Chambersburg PA
CBHW060121230426
43661CB00003B/278